REQUIEM

Poetry books by
Daphne Gottlieb:

15 Ways to Stay Alive
Kissing Dead Girls
Final Girl
Why Things Burn
Pelt

REQUIEM

POEMS

DAPHNE GOTTLIEB

MANIC D PRESS
SAN FRANCISCO

FOR
FRANCES BURTON SILVERMAN
I LOVE YOU

ISBN 978-1-945665-46-2 manicdpress.com
Printed in Canada Cover image: David Jewell

CONTENTS

INTROIT

GRADUAL

ALLELUIA

INTROIT

tapeworm

no one in the world
is waiting for
a poem by me
except you but
I can't write
a poem today.
things got really
dire and weird
all of a sudden.
you hear about things
happening like that:
kisses. lightning.
minds changing.
none of these things
happened to me but
other things did.
mundane, ugly things
having to do with
bodies and pain
and unhappiness
and insurance
companies and bodies
that don't work
and capitalism
that doesn't work
and money
and budgets
and emergencies
that break the budget
and occasions
you have to dress for
and prescriptions
and the rain
and it's hard to write

out from underneath
all the trouble
to find a poem
in all the ugly
and all the pills
that don't work anyway
and that's when
i think about
tapeworms; like
things that come out
of us, things that we need
to get out, like poems.
in the old days, they didn't have
pills so someone like you
or me would fast
for three days until
we were starved and then sit
in front of a glass
of warm milk and the hungry
worm would come out
to eat, inch to foot,
right up the throat
and out the mouth.
i am open-
mouthed in front
of the tapeworm-white
screen. i don't have
a poem but I have warm
milk. something's stirring
inside me.
who knows what
could happen.
i just wanted
to let you know
i'm trying.

my name is pronounced like breaking glass

Peanut butter and government
cheese, city clinic, but also also taxis
and bar tabs and listen:
Suicide bombers are middle-class.
Who else needs something to die for?
What is something to die for
except an excuse to keep living?
I never wanted to be politicized
but then your body. Why you are in danger.
Why you are not. The sheets turned into flags
and the flags turned into blood
and here we are.
The flu is ten times
deadlier than revolution.
Broke is a cold to poor's flu.
The brick is in love with the window.
The brick is in love with air.
The government's phone tap
that clicks on the line
is an angel clucking its tongue
at us. The cat is playing with a moth.
The moth has one leg left, and one
wing. It is so hard
to put things back together. It is so hard
to change, to repair
the world. Love needs gravity.
If the moon was any closer,
I would throw it. I love you so much.
Something's exploding.

poem for the woman at the open mic who read a haiku about unhoused people having sex that ended, "if the shopping cart's a-rocking, don't come a-knocking"

1. You were a teenager.
You had one condom
and nowhere
to go. This
is nothing like that.
Homelessness is transmitted
through body fluids. Through sharing
works. Through kissing, public toilets,
through thought, through seeing.
Don't see it. Don't touch.
Sex is a luxury the way
the moon is a luxury, meaning
that it is always there but it needs
time and space to be yours
and the incontinent man
in the wheelchair, the woman with scabies or lice
whose pants won't zip has no space.
Two men collecting cans before dawn,
arms caked with garbage cans. The immaculate
woman who's working two jobs and sitting up all night
in a drop-in shelter. The man
talking to the moon,
to himself, to God.
God is too busy
to have genitals. God is just
trying to survive. Desire
has no home. Unhoused
people have bodies. Is there love
during wartime and is this
anything else?

2. Nothing was rocking.
There was no door to knock. The woman
was raped. The police report and so what.
Move the body from the center
to the side. Now move the body
farther.
Move it harder, move the body across
the city, move into the shadows,
in police citations, into shelters
or still in the streets,
hands together – the body
stays warmer if it moves.
Move it under blankets.
Hand in hand, it's warmer.
Stay close.
The raped woman is so hot,
she's burning up.
Start again. This is about violence,
not sex, not love,
not the moon, a silver coin
in night's palm, a hand
that can hold and kiss
and in doorways
and alleys
and parks and anywhere else
people will fuck,
there is desire
and sometimes love.

3. Nothing was rocking.
If you got it on you.
The body stays warmer.
Move it into the streets.
Don't come knocking.
Burn it down.

i won't count the stars*

knife

I was sleeping   rugged   when the knife
came   it was   scary dark rough   open-eye
not   sleeping
in the open dark   deer-gutting   dark
I knew   someone would come in small
punctures   cutting red   black
and blue   I thought it would be   a
friend, whose tent   stolen   red
into shreds   by the police   black and blue
they   bone and wood   saw blade gutting hook
to   someone   a   friend
who had no shelter   into shreds nothing   to
sleep on   or the knife   the tent sliced
apart   open   into dumb mouths   call   it
a trophy mount   someone   a light swinging
in the dark   to kill   what
we call home   to   stab   or   slice
and the blade   *Hey*   the light said
You   *Get Up*

vacation

the mangroves   the island pool   I
needed drugs   to get a beautiful place   to wake
up in the morning   in canvas
on the streets   to   refresh   body   and
mind   got   kicked   out   of
a small grocery store   showers   and
electricity   got kicked out of
my apartment   this isn't really camping
lost my job   no place to go

---

*Texts used to create this piece adapted from interviews at "Voices of the Homeless," advertisements for travel and knives, newspaper articles, crime blotters, and legal statutes.

no tourist I needed to decide
where to put the fire and then me
not trusting shelters creature comforts
myself no place to go no tour in the
mangroves or dark sandy beaches
not the island pool
the most famous trail leave my stuff
alone my canvas hotel
room prison home
where I went where did I go
I know where the fire goes and I
know a beautiful place I have
other people I hear them talk I am
woken by their light I can smell their food
and they are watching watching my tent
watching me

repair

the girls around here make a wall
with the body's fluids and salts to make a wall
a good wall someplace safe with a
cooker a lot of the girls down here hold
the barrel can duct tape
can fix anything gotta fix cotton fever
after everything they can fix and stay
against all kinds of bumps bangs
and wear and tear from the law for the
protection when Narcan can't just
know duct tape holds what's
inside in place a lot of the girls get
blood in the barrel move the needle
girls around here can make a really good
duct tape tent fix rips a new
needle if you have duct tape
it's not too late to fix

field medicine

and some of us are   bleeding
and some of us   have bled for this country
            some of us   have risked   our
lives   have not stopped   bleeding
            for this country
if it is full   of money   right now
we do not have   money it is full of dirt
we might smell bad   cleanse the wound
wash with water   this police officer
            these scissors   that knife   police
are searching for   police look at us
police tied the woman   we are   like duct tape
            like filth   the woman we are like
does not deserve
who to report   police to   you know
            I mean come on   police refused
made me   wash with water   made me perform
a sex act   the woman bleeding   was
bleeding   thrown bleeding
into a trash can   here   in this town   you
know   I mean   come on

newspaper

hey   the police   cut a hole   in the tent
I mean it   was a slash   and they used it
as a hole   a fist   was inside   and inside the
fist   the mace inside   they   sprayed
the mace inside they   joked   about it being bear
season we tried to get out   bear maced for
prostitution   or sleeping or stealing   a   k9
unit   the police you know   blunt force
quality   of   life
stab wounds   on the left   trauma
knocked to   the fist   kicked and beat
the police are   felony murder assault

with a deadly   hit and run   I was hit
and run for prostitution   I was   raped
by 3 cops   do   you   know   what
hit me   do you know   his pistol   do
you know   what   the blankets protected
never a damn thing   never a damn thing
and that mace   a badge and a gun   with
bears   contusions   abrasions   the police   a
wooden lot   ID   a ride   stripped me
down   naked   alone   tied with
duct tape   in a trash can   with duct tape in
a parking lot   in the rain   alone
except the bear   there had to be   I wished for
the   bear
to come   to finish it   the duct tape
stuck on its teeth

statute

my hands   through the sleeves   the
familiar routine   he said   and I said   he said
You're   he   said   *You're now*
familiar   *an emergency*
you're the shopping cart   *the body*
stolen   that I could afford   to buy
nail holes   like track marks   my ID
the tent my sleeves   my arms
everything   the body   *you know*
that cart is stolen they said *you can't take it*
so I set it on fire I set my everything   to
ashes   walked   away
my coat on the sidewalk scarf   hat sweater
they squawked   shirt   into   their walkies
pants   nothing
but   my   underwear   and   shoes
nothing   but the skeleton   I left the
cart   the police   behind me

and now the flames   easier to carry ashes
none of it the body   none of it the skeleton
none of it   mine

special summer issue

in the great outdoors   there's a lot of violence
    every time   the cops
bust it down   we want a place soft
and self-repairing   to fix   I wish
  if it was summertime   under the bridge or
someplace   summertime
  toast   some marshmallows   some
place   if we were   someplace   safe
  you know   this dream   alive
duct tape   and a place to live
nerves blood vessels   alive   I think
hair follicles   glands   I think
most of us   if we were someplace
  you can almost   see it   from here
I think most of us want   summertime
want   to   don't you want to   I want
to be   some place   this dream: to not
watch the sunset   to not
    count the stars

crash course

I study the card in front
of me. I strap my body
down. I am told to hide
or get rid of anything
that is not my body.
I might need a tube
on my face or I might need
to float and If the plane punches
the ground, my body needs
to make a letter P:
head to the seat in front of me
hugging my knees.
I know this could end in an inferno,
a cautionary tale my family whispers.
I am prepared to bake in a tin.
I am prepared to survive.
I do not need this
safety position on my flight but
I need it. Sometimes
on the bus. Sometimes at my desk.
In bed every night, I sleep fetal
with my hands clasped under my thighs.
It is how I brace now, how
I learn to pray for a small god
favor. Please send me
an impact that is just
a little bit softer,
with just a little less ash.

GRADUAL

not a nice girl

i am why we can't have
nice things. the stain
on my shirt by noon, the shrapnel
around my desk, the cat

litter punctuating the floor.
i am why we can't need nice.
the tarnish on my shirt
by noon, the fragments of a bomb

around my small table
like a kitten left lying in a public place
is not charming. one need not, cannot, or
does not wish to give a specific name,

a dirty mark for the upper body,
and buttons down the front. at
my highest point, a guilty conscience
is my source of food.

the carnivorous and nocturnal
mark is not seductive.
i am why we can't hold.
there is nothing nice

about authority.
we can't have
polite creatures.
we make war

under the dirty mark
with a single
carnivorous
name.

woo

"Until the 1930s, suitors would present severed heads to potential partners to woo them…" —*The Irish Independent,* report on Taiwanese indigenous peoples

Pour her a glass of wine with the severed head
at the bottom. When she drinks the wine,
she will find the head. Run her a bath
with scented candles and rose petals.
Float a rubber duck
with the head tied to it.
Leave a trail of notes for her with letters cut
from the paper. Use *that* knife.
Blindfold her and take her where you first met.
Use *that* blindfold.
Take champagne. And a glass for the head.
Hire a violinist. Hire a skywriter. Hire a lawyer.
Tell her you got her a gift
to show her how much you love her.
Tell her you want to spend the rest
of your life with her.
Put plastic underneath
so it doesn't stain.
Play "Head," and "Head Like a Hole,"
and "Headhunters." Walk in just after the songs,
holding the head. Have a waiter bring her
favorite dessert with the severed head inside.
Give her a foot massage.
Crown her little toe
with the head. Do it the old-fashioned way.
Do it right. Get down on one knee.
Get all the way down, with one of her hands
between both of yours.
Clench the head between your teeth.

goodbye summer

There is no summer
this year: How it got

cold. If you aren't
saying something. That's all

you need to say. Keep your tongue
in your mouth. Too much summer

on your tongue can turn you. There is no
summer this year. You are all hello

but I am not making lemonade. I am not oiling myself
up. You vacation at the Cape. You send a postcard.

It says. *Not much.* It says. *Having a time.*
You were all hello on me. The postcard in the puddle.

Hello from the Cape. Hello from the Coast.
Hello from the Cake. Hello from the Cunt.

Hello. Hello.
I wish I wish you were here

to break my bed with your lure and line,
but I will not blow up my beach ball

and there is no pollen. The lake is cold
and no one is swimming. I don't care

how hello you are because it is not
summer. I've moved on. Sown and reaped. Built

a fire. Cleaned my house.
There is no summer.

I buried armloads of tomatoes and zucchini
in shallow, sordid graves.

Burned my bathing suit and danced
it into ashes under my flip-flops.

Forked the raft to shreds.

i do not want to fuck you like a poem

i want to fuck you like whatever it is
that makes the birds scatter from the wires
over traffic, all at once.

i want to fuck you like there are angels
tied up in the prayers of birds over traffic
watching us fuck.

i want to fuck you like angels covered in mud
scattering from the wires
like earthworms cut in half
like disaster is sacred
like your name comes
hot and hard on my lips
like mess is a sacrament
like looting is holy
like the sidewalk cracks through the sheer force
of grass and desire.
i want to fuck you like you're a femme and i'm not
like you're healthy and i'm not
like you're catholic and i'm not
like you're scared
like you're smart
like a virgin
like you're cheating
like a rumor
a secret
a psalm.

i want to fuck you like a pilgrimage
like you are the road trip and every wrong turn
like you are a bad neighborhood
like you are mine

i want to fuck you like your teenage car
like a hitchhiker and a 12-pack
fuck you speeding, broken, like a paintslash skyline
fuck you like skidding stars, dead deer and fresh fruit by the roadside
like the radio never stops

i want to fuck you like a hit and run
like body damage
like the jaws of life open and open and more
and more I want to fuck you like the clock is ticking
like the ship is sinking
like the moon is sobbing
like the bomb is falling
like the kingdom is coming
i want to fuck you like we're not in kansas anymore —

i want to fuck you like we're home.

the bullet teaches us how to dance

I want you to know:
When the girl shot herself in the street,
I was not dancing.
I was in the club darkening a corner
or walking lonely home with my heart
balanced on a cigarette tip,
a wounded deer, my chest, staggering
that night, that year, my whole life
that I could not find the girls
whose mouths matched mine,
whose mouths made history
eating fire in the street,
yelling because it felt good
and maybe because it mattered.

The girl in the street knew the difference
between yelling and screaming.
The girl shot herself in the street,
haloed green in the traffic light, painted gold,
detonated like a disco ball,
spilling like a drink and red red red.

She didn't say a thing.
Blood shines black in the dark.
The unhurry of the ambulance lights
floating lazy around and around
her body. Everyone walked away.
scented by brass.

After the bullet, the white chalk halo.
Believe: This was everything she had
left of her, lonely and angry
and rage and gone.

People did not stop dancing.

Let's say we wore the same skin, or wore it differently,
if she was browner or blacker or redder or the geometry
of ribs or the kindness of her swells or mine.
We were not friends.
I did not know her. But maybe
I had seen her,
breathed her in and out
as we panted on the dance floor,
I borrowed her lighter
or maybe rattled spines side by side with coffee
and listened to poets speak like it was the first time
they heard their own voices.

I mean, I didn't know her. I never met her.
I heard her name was Jasmine.

Jasmine, maybe I was looking for you that night,
for someone you had been, someone before
your slow suicide by cigarette, your faster suicide
with the powders and the tar and the spirits
that dragged you forward, a gun in your hand,
into the intersection that night. Jasmine, maybe
I was looking for me.

Blood and guns are the same color in the dark.

Our bodies have always been battlegrounds.

You became your own weapon,
firing through time and space
and me, despite my SOS heartbeat,
my cyanide first girlfriend
and my mayday kisses,
and despite my combat boot coming-out song

over and over in emergency broadcast time
with so much silence instead of a mother,
despite so much that left me barely alive,
I knew that despite all this,
I was lucky,
and lucky goes dancing.

That night, the music did not stop.
When the bar closed,
I was covered in sweat. You were
covered by the tv news. We were both
alone.

Even through the breakbeat, there is the graveyard,
the tyranny of if and when,
like in Seattle, Washington, in 2015,
where a dyke was attacked with
a pocketknife, a dog leash, and a black marker,
or Columbus, Ohio, in 2016, where a woman was shot
and beaten to death
in front of her mother,
and New York City, in 2017,
where a dyke was beaten unconscious
on the subway,
and New York City, in 2018,
where a dyke was beaten
until her spine was fractured
and in Aberdeen, Maryland, in 2019,
where a dyke was shot to death in her driveway,
and Miami, Florida, in 2020, where a dyke's car
was surrounded and she was shot,
and in El Paso, Texas, in 2021,
where a dyke couple
was tortured and shot
and in Chesco, Pennsylvania, in 2022,
when a dyke was shot

by the police and the attorney general
said it was justified,
and in Wynwood, Florida, in 2023,
where a dyke was punched until
she lost consciousness
and that's when I stopped reading the news.

The photo of you was your body
covered with a blanket
was a flare on the street,
was the bar's name in neon. End Up.

Jasmine, your body
was always a battleground,
when you walked to work
or walked home
or walked to a club,
your body and my body,
so near but never against,
bodies that can coil and gasp,
that can recoil and twist
into coffins so easily
at the ends of cigarettes
at the mouths of bottles
and why should those men's violence
come as any surprise?

Jasmine, the gun was pointing the wrong way.
This is not rage.
This is resistance.
This is resilience.
This is ours.
Living well is not the best revenge.
The best revenge is living,
Your lonely

is ours, and we keep
going, so in your name,
I will drag the outlaw of my body
to where it is still illegal,
in the city of junkies
and thieves and whores
and poets, we will dance for you,
lonely ghost. Lost girl.
Dyke.

Jasmine, this is not last call.
We are still calling.
Take the sheet off
your body and rise
from the street.

Come on, Jasmine.
The sun needs to rise.
Let's go to the beach and help.

every other name

There is a tattoo in weird balloon letters that holds your clavicle in place. I could never tell what it said. "*It says, YOU'RE TOO CLOSE,*" you told me, laughing, and you pulled me back down on top of you by my hair. Finally, a reason for hair. I cut it short last time my heart got broken. Now it was down to my shoulders. It grew between and around the nest of your hands, and you kissed me, and I never found out what your tattoo said.

The first line of the song that played the first time you kissed me: *All your dreams are over now*. No one would notice with a kiss like THAT.

That song as prophecy: *You were my favorite moment of a dead century.*

Here's what's in a name: You are that tragic girl in literature, the one who drinks poison then stabs herself. You are a rose by that name, not any other.

Your parents gave you that name. They prayed for you before they cut you off then the machines prayed for you until they were cut off.

Your husband called to see if you were with me. *No,* I said. *Why?*

A rose by any other name. Black tar. China white.

We met in a drug and alcohol counseling class. You told me you were already halfway there: You were an expert on taking drugs. I couldn't take my eyes off you. Even though you were sitting behind me. You had pillows behind you bolstering your bad back. At the first break, we walked outside. I asked you for a cigarette. I'd quit, but where there's smoke, there's you. I'm still smoking, but these days I vape. I'm less toxic than I used to be. That's a joke.

A rose by any other name is roxanol is demerol is sublimaze.

That first date, you brought me home to meet your husband. Your husband, solid and still as a tree, and your son, a portrait of you in boy. We watched TV then you drove me home.

There was too much to say so we said nothing. I didn't dare touch your knee. My eyes didn't stop touching it. You took my hand. The lights on the bridge blushed. Your stereo sang, *You were my favorite moment of a dead century.* It was our song already, and all your wings had fallen down.

You are the kind of beautiful that all feral things are. And borderlines. And dictators. You wear warning like a dress without panties. I fell in love with you because people fall in love. But also this: I made you melt. You, with the bulletproof swagger: I made your knees weak. I made you uncertain. Tender. And I loved how that felt. But I also loved you. The you that had nothing to do with me.

You came over in a black dress, pulled it up over your head like you were a little kid. *Look!* you said. *I wore a dress for you!* You looked down then smiled at me. *And I shaved, too!*

The tattoos on my knuckles say *love poem.* The tattoos on yours say *eat a dick.*

I went to meet you for coffee then trouble. Your hands were shaking. By any other name is methadone is methadose is morphine and you were sweating. The back pain. Your tears were boiling. *It hurts so bad,* you said. I got my coffee to go and took you home to your husband. In your car, the song swam around us. It went, *All your dreams are over now.* It was your song and I learned every note.

You lost a bottle of painkillers. Your doctor was on vacation, you said, and you were fucked. I gave you my two-pill stash and we went to one of the three bad blocks left in the city. I watched you speak your second language: Hug the man then something in your hand. A rose by any other name is crack or meth or anything that could get you through.

You sent me hospital bed peep show photos: Your tits peeking out of your gown, your hips with the gown pulled back like a curtain. And you shaved, too.

A rose by any other name is smack. The scars on your back like you had wings removed. The amateur tattoo over your collarbones. I could never tell what it said. Maybe you told me. Maybe I forgot. The tattoos I kissed that you did yourself during your eighth or ninth rehab. Maybe tenth. You forgot.

Forgotten is not the same as gone. You went missing for four days. Your husband called me. I hadn't seen you.

And more time and more time and still no you and then you called, finally, said you'd relapsed, that you needed to get yourself together, to regroup, to make everything simple for us again. I thought you meant *us*. You meant your husband and your son. You meant not me. When you dumped me, I was staring at the park. The park was built on an old cemetery. I listened to our song. It told me *Your heart can't grieve.*

Your husband called me after a month, after a year, after a year and a half. No, I hadn't seen you.

I was watching the park out the window when you said you needed me. You came over. Or, someone did. A smaller woman with a cane and broken glasses and a sideways mouth and whose hair was mad scientist, not Peter Pan. You were starving, you said. Did I have any food? Could you have a shower? You looked at me looking at you, you, on the verge of panic, your heart laid bare. *Do I really look that bad?*

Slower now, clean and fed, you told me about the rapes, about turning tricks, about the hundreds of turned tricks, the tricks that turned bad, about being held hostage by the man who was later in the papers, the serial killer, about roxy, norco, perco, *Tell me,* I said, but your eyes closed and you slept. Or nodded out.

I'm not using, you said. *I haven't gotten high today.* But you were using. *No,* you said, *I'm just exhausted.* You were using. And you didn't bring any for me. Maybe you were using me. All night next to you, I watched you pull handfuls of hair out of your head. You pulled fitfully, angrily. Once in a while, I stroked the back of your neck, helpless. When the light outside was watery, you got up to pee and limped to the front door and then through.

And then no one could find you again and I called your name to my computer screen, drew your face on every milk carton. Days or weeks or months later, your husband called me and said *I just want to see her one more time before she dies* and online they said *junkie addict whore* and your husband sent a text to a strange number in case you were there, and a text came back: *Yeah, she's here, she's sucking my dick* and your husband asked me had I seen, would a rose by any, and I told him this: I fell in love with you at first sight.

You have the same name as the tragic imaginary girl who drank poison and then stabbed herself. Your hips and legs bloomed in bluish bruises where you stabbed and missed the femoral. You had to go for the femoral or whatever you could get. Your arms were shot.
I'm still in love with you. You are the rush like assault, stealing my breath hard until I double over, and nothing else is even close. It's love. Your tattoo: *If you can read this.*

You can't read the future, chemical toxic, when you will steal money from me and burn holes in my blanket with your crack pipe, when furious and withdrawing, you scream into my voicemail, *You think you're so much better than me.* I don't. That was you.

You drink poison, but I can only dab it behind my ears. You stab yourself, but I can only deep throat the knife. You shoot when I snort.

You hurt yourself harder than me. You die faster. Am I romanticizing this? Probably. But this is a romance. A necromance. Formaldehyde smells so sweet. And before the hospital machines pray over you while one organ follows another into the dark and your heart your heart your heart, years before that, you arise from the dead out of the streets from an apartment two blocks from mine and you tell the internet: *I am alive.*

Start the song over. Sing along, *wrecking and ravaging, savoring savaging.*

Alive. Start here. Be alive with me. Leave the hospital gown and your failed organs and the death certificate behind. Leave the diagnoses and the dimebags, leave the shame and be alive with me. I have nothing for you to rip off except two norco and my Slits tee shirt that you were always trying to steal anyway. Come get them. Come get the rest of you. You are forgiven or you don't have to be. You are not the girl with the poison and the dagger. You are not the poison. Maybe you are the poison. I don't care. Arise. Arose. Come take these flowers I got for you. Come take the rose of my mouth by every other name like curses and kisses and prayers and make everything glow bloody red. We will make every rose blush. I need you. Get well. I love you. Come back.

Goodbye.

ALLELUIA

why white women knit*

When we were growing up, my grandmother
used to knit sweaters for my sister and me.
The open end of a noose is called a honda.

The plain end of a noose is the hitch.
When I was 12, my grandmother
taught me how to pull loops

through other loops, crochet,
the catshank, the monkey's fist.
Having two children

can be accomplished by machine.
The death of a person is called a hitch.
I moved onto purling.

I moved onto fruit for the crows to pluck.
A capitalist would sell you the rope
to hang him, sell the sisal

with the stake. A dog shank
is a sheepshank for free-ended rope.
The rope shall be examined in any open area in front

of the carpet,
the fireplace, the crowd.
I was trying to quit

and needed something
to keep my hands busy.
A hank is uncoiled yarn

rounded into a loop
by mob. Any act of violence
crafted by hand is a lark head

hanging from the popular tree
in my grandma's yard.
She used to knit

neck warmers.
She smelled like
magnolia, sweet and fresh.

When the rope was thrown above,
it got hooked up with the branch,
the limbs, the head,

blood on the leaves. Late at night,
I would come by with my yarn
and decorate the torso

with a love knot,
granny knot,
noose.

---

*All text from Wikipedia entries on knots, crocheting and knitting, various knitting websites, a magician's rope trick website, and the lyrics of "Strange Fruit."

the insurance policy

We earned this. We worked hard.
So tax the body.
Some lives matter more.
That's just the way it is.

You want to be nothing?
Do nothing.
We took the kids to the Grand Canyon that year.
When I exhale, I harmonica.

Home, home on the range. My
husband's teeth in a glass, some
strange science.
You want to be nothing?

There is a man
beating a woman in the street but
I can only hear her. There was a campfire
20 years ago. There is a house

burning down. I brought marshmallows
and chocolate. I brought a forest.
I forgot the matches.
All I'm asking for is a little spark,

a little heat. When I reach for him in the dark
in bed in this house we worked for, he pushes
my hands away. I am probably dreaming. It is cold.
There is yelling on the forest street. My robe
pulls me to the rocks and it flickers. It's my fault. I forgot

the twigs. Am I in the right key? I would have done anything
for my children. My harmonica plays loud,
this lonely. I found the graham crackers.

My bones like twigs. It wasn't supposed to be
like this. The phone has no
cord. Where did I go? My hands hold
each other. Outside, it's raining
ashes. We paid our taxes.

We loved those trips.
My husband is snoring.
Everything is burning
out in the street.

arraignment*

I don't even wait.   I pull her rohypnol off   I shove her
against the quaalude   you can   valium   anything   grab
them   the whisky   ketamine   grab her   to be quiet
to move   to say   she didn't really   move   or say much

ecstasy of the girl   I was on   I took her   I gave her
GHB and   roofies quaaludes whisky   I gave her   I gave her
ecstasy   I gave it to her   good   mushroom inside her
having ether   my ketamine   in her chloroform   her
motionless ativan   her body

she loved it, OK?   I had her   lying ambien like this
rozeram on her back   her mouth is hash   open so I   wax it
it fentanyl   amazing   she did not   klonopin   a muscle
I didn't wear   a zyprexa   i ataraxed in her   three times
she was

crying but she didn't   malibu   she said she liked   liquored she said

  it was very   versed   very seconal   very sexy   to be
raped.

*All text from Michael Briggs, Bill Cosby, Donald Trump, reddit, and the *Physicians' Desk Reference*

the trial*

I was not in the wrong of my throat did I nothing wrong. I did not speak.
All night, how they treated me like a rag doll, like garbage,
These men, impotent men, parasites, cyphers, entered my home.
My head struck the headboard of the bed and I fell forwards.

All night, how they treated me like a rag doll, like garbage,
downwards on the pillow with gaping mouth and staring.
My head struck the headboard of the bed and I fell forwards.
They were indescribably fierce and frenzied, amusing themselves.

Downwards on the pillow with gaping mouth and staring —
please remember how the world implodes, how I am a field of ruins.
They were indescribably fierce and frenzied, amusing themselves.
I speak now, at gunpoint, to rebuild whatever is necessary.

Remember how the world implodes, how I am a field of ruins.
I was not coquettish and untidy. I was sacrificed.
How I speak now, at gunpoint, to rebuild whatever is necessary.
I have so much to say, I don't know where to start.

---

*All text from Gisele Pelicot and *Les Miserable*'s Fantine, who has no last name

appeals*

I'm nothing   but part pleasure   part addiction   that's love   how
we depress   "release"   the shutter   without thinking
just shooting   using both hands   coming inside   focus

the tripod and   a better grip   hope   not fear:
steady hands   but also   insurance   because love is a dead
end   is the wave   up to your eye   that naked island   I
hold back   the right settings   against her knowledge

men used to come   into my house   into the room   my wife
my little girl   in my heart   a memory   without
blur   start somewhere   my heart beating unforgivable   a
laugh that loses   on an aperture   I had needs   the lips
the important first things   ask for forgiveness   just shooting
that naked   unforgivable   heart

---

*All text from Gisele Pelicot with camera manual and famous French love songs

oui the people

French, English and Spanish are cognates, meaning
we split off from the same ancient language,
divided like continents and consonants.

In every culture, our first word is usually *mama*.
The first words we learn in any other
language are curse words. The word for
motherfucker in French Is *connard*.
In French, one word for fuck is *baisir*.
In English, it is *fuck*. In America,

the first thing men know about sex
is a stain. The first thing women learn
about sex is blood. The first thing girls
learn about birth control is to cross their legs.
Most of us learn about sex
from our parents. Children learn to count
after age four. My mother taught me

that if you get raped, *oh well. It happens.*
Get over it. In France, Gisele Pelicot's husband
drugged her and had her raped
by more than 80 men.
Un, deux, troix, quatre. It happens.
Memories begin to form at the age

of two or three. Quatre. Cinq.
My mother would not let me
take Spanish. My mother
wanted me to learn French.
She was from Belgium. I do not
know anything about Belgium
other than horses and chocolates.
In English, we say *hung like a horse.*

We confuse chocolate with romance.
We confuse anatomy with scale.

The first word I said was *no*.

The first word I spelled was *stop*.

The first time I was raped, alcohol
was also in my body. The last time, it was
a drink with roofies and GHB. In between,
too many mornings without memories,
waking up with my clothes still on,
with my clothes on wrong,
bra inside out or underwear missing,
bruises like cave paintings.
A night not to remember.

To say sex in French is *baisir*, but that also
is the verb for *kiss*. To say *motherfucker*,
you must say *niquer*, which also is used
for being fucked over, being screwed.
It happens. Get over it. The equivalent
to asshole or dickhead is *ducon*.
English and French appear
side-by-side in legal documents
One word appears next to its translation:
Aiding and abetting. Free and clear.
Last will and testament.

In America, we say *rape*.
We say *consent* in the culture but
ignore it in the courts.
In France, they say *violence,*
coercion, threat or surprise.
No one says *justice*.

Spanish is also a cognate.
It is also a romance language.
Isn't it romantic? The rate of rape
is lower than the rate in France
which are both lower than America's.
If I learned Spanish instead,
would things be different?
I saw women dancing
under spacious skies, folding
their arms into the Macarena.
This song says *Give your body joy.*
So much is lost in translation.
Why can't it be that simple
to be *gratis, libre, free?*
Don't crown our good
with motherhood.
Guarantee us
our bodies from *si*
to shining *si.*

TRACT

everyone falls

Today is my cat's birthday.
She is nineteen. I do not know
how long I can grow her.

I have turned two cats
to ash with my love.
There are days

I want to set myself on fire
and run into the street screaming,
I AM STILL CULTURALLY RELEVANT!

I smoked
for 25 years and then
quit. There is nothing

more frightening than
a middle-aged woman
who wants.

Dear Miss Gottlieb,
I am a high school
student and I am performing

your work. What year were you
born? Was it after 1960? Sometimes
I see my dead friends

on the street. I have passed
the age where excess
is the killer, or tall buildings

or gorges or razors or bridges.
Now people die

of diseases. *Dear Ms. Gottlieb,*
I am a poet just starting out. What
advice do you have
for me?

Don't. *Dear Ms. Gottlieb,*
1968: Lyndon B. Johnson, the Vietnam War
Frankie Lyman overdosing on heroin.

Dear Ms. Gottlieb, You will never win
the MacArthur, the Guggenheim,
the Kentucky Derby. 1968: MLK shot.

Civil Rights Act. White Album.
Dear Ms. Gottlieb,
Your bikini days are over

unless you are making
a statement. Are you making
a statement? Are you making

a scene? There is nothing
more obscene than middle-aged
desire. *Are you going to go*

quietly? We can do this
the hard way. I have a friend
who is sixty.

I have buried
both my parents.
I will never

have children.
I have a friend
who is sixty.

Her cat just died.
For her birthday,
she jumped

out of an airplane.
The view, she said.
She landed

safely. She landed
on land. I land on
metaphor. My whole life

is already about watching
the end rush up at me
too fast, nowhere I thought

I'd be. 1968: Martin Luther King Jr.,
Helen Keller
Robert Kennedy

Before she jumped,
they told my friend
that some people

pee themselves
on the way down,
some people

black out oh
it's so fast
and everyone falls.

playing chicken

any romance
is a breakup movie if
you watch it backwards or
just stop in the right place.
the lion roars
after a break up. one man

jumpcut other man then back,
both of them stuck face down to
cars. someone's foot inside puts
the hammer down, hurtles the men
face-first at each other.

it is what i need to see:
unhappy lives. suffering.
people without options.
it's very late in the film.
they are playing chicken. which
came first, my heart or yours?

they are playing chicken. movie
endings don't change. they all have
endings. we have an ending.
even before you are gone,
i know the loss. loneliness

grows in me like tumors. i hatch them
like tiny chicks. peep. peep.
i gather them in my arms,
keep them clean and feed, keep them
safe. they are not alone. i tell them,

you are not alone. you
are chicks. they laugh.
i tell them about the game

named after them:
men on cars propelled towards each
other. there is danger in
getting close. the chicks
learn to strut. they are
chicks. they have no use

for cars. *no one wins,*
i tell them. *trust me.*
this isn't my first chicken
coop. I scatter seed. I put out
water. *keep your eyes peeled,*
I say. *playing chicken is fun*

until it's not. get
ready. you never know
what's going to
happen when a fox
shows up hungry.

yahrzeit

My mother, whose face, feet, hands, made mine in her image.
That is rarely what people mean when they say
I am my mother's daughter.

My mother was her mother's daughter. Her mother walked
a cheetah on a leash.

Her mother died dancing on a table. Her mother was a model.
She became an actress-model.

My mother, the actress, and her father's instructions to take a seat
on the casting couch so she might make it.

My mother, who could say my name and have it sound exactly like
shame on you.

My mother, flapping in with a beach towel when the tooth fairy
forgot to come.

She wrote to me: *I am, as you seem to think, ready to leap tall
buildings in a single bound for you.*

My mother, whose mother died when she was nine, my mother
whose traveling salesman father grew her in boarding school. My
mother who tried to be a mother without having one.

And when I talk about my mother, I am, of course, also talking
about me. Something of me died, too. Something is still dying.

My mother would not let me take Spanish, go trick-or-treating, join
the Girl Scouts, get my ears pierced, or own Barbie dolls.

My mother, who loved me enough to throw her body between me
and my father during assaults, but never loved me enough to leave
him.

My mother sometimes laughed backwards: *ah ah ah ah ah.*

Swooping in, my mother rips me away from my homework into some kind of ersatz jitterbug, whipping me around the room to Carly Simon, then Foreigner, then David Bowie and Talking Heads.

My mother, whispering to me to go and change, to hide the outfit my father wouldn't let me out of the house in under the seat in the car, and change when I get there.

My mother, not letting me out of the house in *that.*

Under God says the Pledge of Allegiance. My mother says *No. We are not under "God."* I learn to move my lips silently to avoid the principal. For my mother, I killed God.

It's very flattering, but isn't it enough already? she would say. *I mean, 20 years.* She would be smiling softly. She might stroke my hair.

Hang in there, Mom, I'm almost done. I promise I'll stop tomorrow: your scotch on the rocks and Pall Malls.

My mother at 60, dancing on a bar on New Year's Eve.

Mom, I said. You were dancing on the bar? *Every time I raised my arms,* she said, *my dress creeped up to my waist. It was a great night.*

I am, as you seem to think, she said, *ready to cure your cold over the telephone.*

I'm sorry, Mom. You probably knew I was going to do this.

During chemotherapy, she woke up and took my hand. She whispered, *not with a bang, but with a...* Her eyes filled with tears and then they closed and then she was asleep again. Or pretending to be.

My mother putting in her upper plate when she was days from death so that the married man she was been dating won't see her without them. *You'd better kiss her,* hisses my aunt from outside the room.

During chemotherapy, my mother whispered, *Tell me again about the rabbits, George.* I can't. All the ways I failed you. The bullet to the back of the skull.

Not with a bang.

You always have to put a twist on it so it hurts, don't you? It's already twisted, Mom.

She always gets the last word. She said, *I am, as you seem to think, always ready to put on face so that you follow in the path.*

I follow and I follow. Sooner or later, I might catch up.

OFFERTORY

why it is so hard to make soup

a soulmate. there must not
be one. i must not have one.
all I ever wanted was
a happily ending-never,
a not-ending, a whisper
at night, a not-alone that is better
than alone even though alone
is not bad, not usually; if love is like you
and your shadow, maybe
i am the girl with no shadow
or rather maybe i am just
the shadow, a stain of light
through a flower petal, everything
left that the sun can't kill.

a shadow, some slight chance
of me, no chance of not-ending up
killed by words, what was made
in kisses and gestures and soft
hope, light through a flower's petals

loves me

loves me not

you pulled too hard

slight chance of ever
wanting you back
i want you back
i don't want you back
i really don't
i just want a chance
a shadow of a chance

of ever finding that world
again, a *let's go on vacation*
or *sorry you're sick, here's soup*
i know you hate soup but here's soup
or *let's go to brunch*
or *damn you're beautiful*

or just

i love you

not knowing when i'll hear

i love you

again, when the next kiss
will come, no more middle
of the night too crowded in the bed,
your arm and my leg
and the dog somewhere and you pull me
closer and i close my eyes

i fall asleep like i fall in love
too fast too hard
they say it's not the fall
that kills you because
you fall right into the soulmate's arms
you knock them over
until they are made of blood and shadows
they die a hero, you live
and everyone wins

i'm always so tired
too tired to win or swim
upstream in soulmating season
too many shadows in my head

made of other shadows like
stories made of other stories
made of kisses and gestures
and soft hope that night

the stories went marching up
and up one by one went two
by two, up the ramp, that plank, that night
i tripped on the dark
i fell off the ark
saw the slightest shadow
on the side of that ship

enter the villain

Turns out I'm not the villain after all,
but it's too late to change my mind. Who knew
it would be like this, with riot perfume
and someone else's hate? My fatal
soundtrack. My inconvenient latex clothes.
It's not all invisibility cloak
and death ray, henchmen and perfect
hair. The people vowel, torches in the air,
ignite. I am the future they want,
but they don't care. They melt and rip my cape.
I don't want Gotham. I don't want headlines.
All I've ever wanted is an honest
love by my side and maybe a baby
in my arms. How do you find the right
Heaven? Let me meet my maker
like this: full of love and
the detonator button in my hand.

no hope

No Hope! See? That's what gives me guts. —The Minutemen

Gandhi was noble / noble Gandhi said / when the Jews were rounded up / were killed / were inevitable / he said they should've just suicided / it would've been noble, he said / I say, dead is dead / me, I would rather be alive / than noble / and maybe you, too / the open mouth of a gun can say the same thing to a German / as a Jew / 6 bullets to a chamber / it takes one to kill a Jew / make 5 for the Nazis first / dead is dead and if I was going to die anyway / take 5 / take a child / I was a child / my mother told me / about when she was a child / escaping the Nazis / I read the story of the child / that girl / how she hid in the attic / how she wrote a book / how she died / as a child / I heard about the ballerina / how she danced for the Nazis / and how she shot them / I wanted to be a ballerina / who writes a book /

since I was a child / I was told that violence is / violence is wrong / but when the state's agents are / executing you / isn't it self-defense / against killers / terrorists / 3000 people dead / September / 2001 / in New York / america is the home of the brave / america what did you do / you fight fire with fire / what do you fight terror with / when you make it / gaza and afghanistan and iraq / korea and haiti /romania and somalia / the defacement in moscow / Idaho/ of a synagogue / the armed uniforms killing unarmed black men / the woman in a chain store / an american / being told that / in america / she will be hung with her hijab / the vietnamese-american woman / pumping gas / being told by a man / american / to *get the fuck out of my country* / high school boys chanting *WHITE POWER* marching down / the school hallway / left / left / right / right / right / a woman's breast grabbed on the subway / the man claimed it was his right /

wings spreading / all wrong / in america / the new country rising / this old forgotten country / this country never tried to kill us / with kindness / and here we are with the mouth of an american /

gun / trying to stop it / turn this over inside out / to point their hate in the right direction / it is so easy to feel lost / helpless / powerless / to fall into depression / to fight the blue / what do you fight the blue with / blue like rain / wet / it's not water in that shower / I've been told / I know / I've heard / depression

is rage turned inward / turn this over / inside out / to make something happen / to believe and change / is to make change happen / is noble / really noble / we can't do it alone / maybe with someone else / and if not / then maybe with someone else and someone else / and if not / then maybe / us / coming with a book of matches/ open the white

to the brown and red / are you ready to / strike / are you ready / you have to be ready / turn blue inside out / it is orange / and orange and blue are flame / are warm / move fast / there is no water in those showers / there is no america / but there is us / and we can write a book like a little girl / we can america like / we are free / come on / let's dance like we / made it out of the attic / alive

water works

You ask me for words of hope. Spells don't work. They are only signs. The sign for change is in a math is a delta. The mouth of a river is a delta. Put that glass of water up to your mouth and drink. Let's say they world is melting. Let's say this is what we've got, what's left. Raise your glass.

Ice caps race against each other, polar caps melt. Penguins wear bikinis instead of tuxes, oh adaptation, the fab spring line and the sea is rising, is rising to see the bikinis, is rising to see the creatures on land, is shaking its head at us.

The ocean is kind of a wet blanket. The ice sheet over Antarctica, that wet blanket, could cover the United States twice. Could smother the United States. Smothering is drowning, except without water.

The ocean likes pounding things to sand, smashes the shore for hourglasses on end. The water has got time to kill.

It will outlast human cruelty. It will rise on the strong dead angry arms of the Middle Passage. Fuck the Titanic.

Which spreads faster, fire or water? You fight fire with fire. What do you fight water with? Nothing. You don't bother. You can't win. The sea level creeps up. Some think the world will end in fire. From what I've tasted of desire. Take a cold shower. Take a bath. Drink up. It only takes 2 tablespoons of water to drown. Watch the hourglass. Watch the sea level.

The glass is half full. Drink water. Piss it out. Let the ocean move through you. The water is running. It's time to go. The bad blue sea will push us up, up in a rush, higher and higher. We will move together, us and the ocean, faster and faster, rising giddy. If we can get high enough, we're gonna kiss the sun.

COMMUNION

my dog teaches me things

rescue

He is made of sticks and sorrow. A dead owner and his mother and sister and no food. His body is testimony that he wasn't treated well. The volunteer brings him to me, and his legs are stiff as twigs. He does not know where he is. He does not know what is going on. He has lost his home, his teeth, his name, whatever it was, his sister, his mother. Under my hands, the toothpick architecture of his body relaxes. I pull him closer. It is like he has washed up on shore, limp and almost drowned in trauma. He puts his head on my chest and sighs and closes his eyes. I am falling in love so I say, *I'm not sure.* I am falling in love so I say, *I can't /*
I don't know how to do this. He is three pounds. It takes so little to change the whole world.

patient studies

Dog is on my lap. The adoption volunteer is reading all the notes on dog to me. They are like side effects on a medicine bottle. May cause. Some patients experience. Contact your doctor if. The volunteer says *toothless, heart murmur, luxating patellas, disintegrating irises, humpback from scoliosis, hops like a bunny, cataracts* – dog snorts. *You humans have so many words for perfect health,* he says. The volunteer drones on – *constipation, foreshortened foreskin* – The dog taps his foot. He is ill, impatient. *This place smells like a vet,* he says. *Let's get out of here.*

feisty

His name is Feisty, the volunteer says. *He has a sister named Bitsy and a mother named Birdy and his name is Feisty.*

My name is not Feisty, says Feisty, his eyes not leaving the floor. *Feisty this,* says the volunteer. *Feisty that, Feisty, Feisty*. He is shaking with rage and trauma. I put my hand on his head. He puts his head on my chest. And we go home. *Home is not a place,* he mutters. *Home is a name. Being called by your own name.*

Then let's go home, I say. *Let's work on the name.* He looks up at me and there is a flicker of something new there. It fades quickly but it's something Feisty.

coming back

Dog eats. Dog sleeps. And one day when I have been away but I have come back, he runs in a circle to greet me, stamps his feet and sneezes as punctuation. His eyes are stars and warm summer darkness. The kind that feel like love. *Hello,* he says. *I am Doomsday Honeymoon.* Doomsday Honeymoon? *Yes. Doomsday Honeymoon. I chose it myself. It means, There is love at the end of the world.*

running gag

Most people don't know that dogs tell jokes. Dogs don't use words or sound, though. They tell silent jokes, and they're uncharacteristically subtle for dogs.

Dog begins cracking jokes, cocking his head to one side, ears up. He slaps his front feet down and looks up at me. *Well*? I ask. He wags his tail at me. And he is laughing, and he laughs again, and he sneezes again and almost falls down. Now I'm laughing, too, and when I look up, dog is not laughing. *What?* I ask. *I love you,* dog says. *I love you too, but what?* I say.

Dog is hemming and hawing and finally says, *Well, some folks can tell a joke and some folks can't,* collecting his legs under him to sprint to run. He thinks I'm going to chase him. I'm going to chase him. He pushes off from inside the dog bed, leaping into the air, his laugh trailing behind him. *Stop me,* he shouts over his shoulder, *if you've heard this one before.*

working like a dog

From the first, dog comes to work with me. Dog is very popular. We work with people who have less than anyone except each other. They look at my dog with curiosity, with his hanging-out tongue, his sticking-out ribs, his bunny hop. They look at my dog with curiosity and then love. They speak this dialect of dog. No one except me ever expresses self-pity.

I ask dog about this. *I can't really explain about self-pity because I don't really understand it. I can't explain about humans. But for dogs it is like this: There is only now. There is only this. We can only be here.*

Here, he says, flinging his head against my shoulder. *Right here.* He smiles and looks into my eyes. I have never loved now so much.

nothing to say, glad you are here
We start a normal and it goes on and on, richer and thicker towards sundown, a delight so habitual, it is familiar as a light switch in a darkening world. Every day and the possibility of blossoming into good, he rolls on his back and closes his eyes in pleasure when his chest is rubbed. *Good morning.* It is so wonderful, I never take it for granted. Good morning.

love bites
Dog objects to every potential sweetheart I find. *This one's too big,* sniffs dog. *This one's too small.*

Dog growls at anyone trying to kiss me, bites their noses when we're lying down, wriggles between me and anyone trying to curl up with me. *Don't worry,* he says. *I'm here to protect you.*

He pees on one suitor's clothes. He is exiled to the living room. He screams like he is being dismembered. He is allowed back on the bed. He basks in the awkwardness, oversees in case I might need his help. He referees from the corner of the bed, smirking.

blue notes
Sing more, says dog. When he has been hurt or scared or seized or stroked, I have sung to him. I have sung, struggling back tears so tears don't flood him, so the fear doesn't seize him through my chest. Since singing and tears can't happen at the time, because

Sing more, he says, because time and again, he has struggled back to me through broken songs and gasping phrases and pause, I sing for him. *My funny valentine,* I sing, *sweet comic valentine.*

Sing more, he says. *What is good in pain is better in joy.* So I sing.

He closes his eyes and nuzzles against me and smiles.

salty dog
Dog's heart is failing. *Can't they find a better name for it,* says dog. *Maybe heart lullaby, since the heart is soothed from hard beats to a quieter song? Okay.*

Dog's lungs are filling with fluid, the vet says. Salt water, says dog. *We are mostly salt water. Did you know, he says, that the closest relatives dogs have on earth are whales? Whales came up, became dogs, and the whales stayed back in the ocean. Why would I be afraid of a little water? I am going home to the ocean. I am going home to the sea.*

His boat won't hold me. Water wings won't help. There is no way to stop the tides. Fuck you, moon. Fuck you.

time balm
Dog's lungs are filling with fluid. We don't have much time. I ask him: *What is your idea of the best day ever?* I want to make that day. He is in my arms. *Today,* he says. *Today*. He is sleepy, nuzzling into my armpit where he thinks nothing bad can find him. That night, he eats sushi and we go to sleep together, him in my arms. The next night, we eat barbecue. We take a bath and dog tries to drink the bath, then puts his nose in the air and sways like a reed. His legs drift out slowly in the salt water and he floats with his head on my chest. Today.

not the end
I sing to him. *You are my sunshine, my only sunshine. Please don't take my sunshine.* His eyes are locked in mine, I hold him, gaze back.

Then his pupils blow wide and he is gone. *Away.*

From the stars, back to the stars.

My dog star.

Away.

in case you ever need it, it is here

this is yours.
rip this from the book
or make a copy.
fold it in half
and half again
and put it in your wallet
or between the mattress and box spring
or taped on the belly of your desk
so it is there if

and if:
what happened
to your body
to your head
to your heart
is not your fault.
you did not cause this.
you did not deserve this.

i wish i could make this more
poetic. this is the best I can do.

you can't take the blame for someone
smashing your hand with a hammer:
their tool, their swing, your hand.
(if you're the one with the hammer,
please put it down. let it go back to sleep
under the kitchen sink. let this now be over.)

water your plants.
the alive want to stay alive.
the body, brain, heart
try to live. they know how to knit back
together. it takes pain and time,

but they get there. let them suture
and secure. let the white coated mechanics
do what they do. they'll take it
but give it back.

your body is yours.
it will always be yours.
you are not the sum
of what happened to you.
your whole life
is not this. will not be this.
you do not speak
a language made of rape and this
is not your name.

let your name be
the name of you, who can
do the unthinkable:
stand up. keep moving.
Take a shower or eat
breakfast, go to classes or
find ways. all ways.
keep going and keep going

or pull the covers back
over your head and try again
tomorrow. It's okay. you
are doing impossibly hard things and you
are doing them. keep going
and summer will find you.
the smell of fresh-cut grass will
tell you it's summer. peaches and hope.
laugh because you are surviving. rage.
open your mouth and your fists.
tell the truth. tell a friend. listen
to their heart. it's beating the same

miracle as yours.
when wounds heal, they scar.
our newest skin is shiny,
strongly pigmented or pale white,
glimmering history.

Scars are the stories we win,

be all the shiny glitter
you need.

rise from it
like ashes.

ACKNOWLEDGMENTS

Thanks to Manic D for picking up what I was putting down. This book owes a huge debt to Alex Dark and Kimberly Dark, as well as the rest of the Writes of Spring writers, who helped this book rise from ashes near Dolores Park. Blessings to the hardest workers on this book, Moshpit Perestroika, Tchotchke Dentata, and Doomsday Honeymoon, who sat tirelessly on my lap over a decade until it was done.

"I won't count the stars" previously appeared in a slightly different form in *Colossus: Home.* "goodbye summer" and "poem for the woman who read a haiku…" previously appeared in *Flicker and Spark: A Contemporary Queer Anthology of Spoken Word and Poetry.* "in case you need it, it is here" appeared in *Courage: Daring Poems for Gutsy Girls.*